D1305788

THIS BOOK BELONGS TO

_____

name

EXTINCT FOR 65 MILLION YEARS, THEY'RE BACK!

Jurassic Park is a totally unique "zoo" located on Nublar Island, about 125 miles (200 km) off the coast of Costa Rica, in Central America. The fulfillment of five years work, is a dream come true for John Hammond, a businessman who made his fortune creating theme parks and zoos around the world.

Imagine an island covered with lush vegetation and inhabited by . . .
LIVE DINOSAURS!

HOW JURASSIC PARK BEGAN

First, paleontologists discovered dinosaur-age fossil mosquitoes (blood-sucking insects) preserved in chunks of amber. The insects' stomachs still contained the preserved blood of dinosaurs they bit more than 65 million years ago. Genetic scientists were then able to remove the ancient dinosaur DNA (the genetic code that acts as a blueprint for creating life) and, with the help of powerful computers, they created living dinosaur embryos.

Dinosaurs are a group of ancient reptiles that lived on the Earth long before human beings appeared. No one had ever seen a living dinosaur before . . . until now!

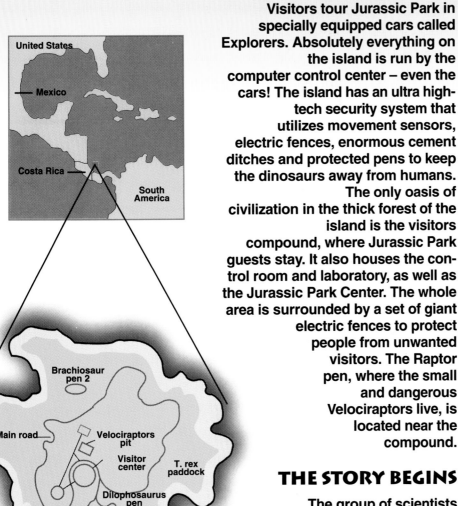

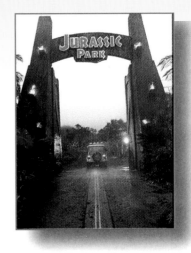

Visitors tour Jurassic Park in specially equipped cars called Explorers. Absolutely everything on the island is run by the computer control center – even the cars! The island has an ultra high-tech security system that utilizes movement sensors, electric fences, enormous cement ditches and protected pens to keep the dinosaurs away from humans.

The only oasis of civilization in the thick forest of the island is the visitors compound, where Jurassic Park guests stay. It also houses the control room and laboratory, as well as the Jurassic Park Center. The whole area is surrounded by a set of giant electric fences to protect people from unwanted visitors. The Raptor pen, where the small and dangerous Velociraptors live, is located near the compound.

THE STORY BEGINS

The group of scientists and visitors arriving at Jurassic Park are about to be the first to tour the park and see living dinosaurs, before the official opening.

The weather is beautiful now, but a tropical storm is heading for the island at lightning speed.

Everything seems fine, but things are about to go very wrong . . .

THE JURASSIC PARK VISITORS

HERE ARE THE EIGHT CHARACTERS WHO WILL EXPLORE JURASSIC PARK WITH YOU

DR. ELLIE SATTLER

Dr. Ellie Sattler is a paleobotanist, a scientist who studies fossil plants. She's come to Jurassic Park to assist Dr. Grant with the inspection.

TIM

Tim is the nine-year-old grandson of John Hammond. A big dinosaur buff, he's on the island to visit his grandpa — and Dr. Grant, his hero.

DR. ALAN GRANT

Dr. Alan Grant, a paleontologist who studies the skeletons and behavior of carnivorous dinosaurs, has been invited to Jurassic Park to inspect the facilities before the official park opening.

JOHN HAMMOND

John Hammond is a billionaire business-man who accomplished his dream to build Jurassic Park. Totally obsessed by dinosaurs, he has invented a new kind of theme park. His company, InGen Corporation, created Jurassic Park and all its dinosaurs.

ALEXIS (LEX)

Lex is Tim's
12-year-old sister.
She's as crazy about
computers as Tim
is about dinosaurs,
and she has a crush
on Dr. Grant.

DR. IAN MALCOLM

Dr. Ian Malcolm is a
mathematical genius
here to inspect the
operations. However,
he doesn't believe that
science can always
control complex natural
systems.
He's certain that
something will
eventually go wrong
with the park.

ROBERT MULDOON

Robert Muldoon is
the island game
warden. Although
he's worked with
dangerous wild
animals for years,
he doesn't trust the
dinosaurs —
especially the
Velociraptors.

DENNIS NEDRY

Dennis Nedry
programmed all the
computer systems in
Jurassic Park. He secretly
decided to sell frozen
dinosaur embryos to a
rival company
for a lot of money.
To sneak the embryos off
the island, he uses the
computer to turn off the
Jurassic Park
security system.
Unfortunately, his
program eventually shuts
down all island control
systems. Now none of the
electric fences are opera-
tional and the dinosaurs
will soon discover that
they can escape!

NOW, IT'S TIME TO MEET ONE OF THE INHABITANTS OF JURASSIC PARK . . .

Lex, Tim and Dr. Grant are walking through the forest trying to find their way back to the visitors center. Last night, they had the fright of their lives, barely escaping a terrifying attack by the Tyrannosaurus rex.
Suddenly, Dr. Grant notices a white patch on the ground under a tree. Looking closer, he realizes it's a nest – but no ordinary nest. Those are dinosaur eggs!

GALLIMIMUS

Meaning of name:
Fowl Imitator

Lived: 67 to 70 million years ago

Meat-eating, Saurischian dinosaur

Family Ornithomimidae

Found in Asia (with a close relative called
Struthiomimus in North America)

First discovered in the 1960s in the southern region
of the Mongolian People's Republic

Scientifically described by Dr. H. Osmolska, Dr. E.
Roniewisz and Dr. R. Barsbold in 1972

Maximum known body size:
17 feet / 5 meters long,
8 feet / 2.7 meters tall

Skull length:
1 foot / 0.30 meters long

Weight:
1,000 lbs / 450 kg

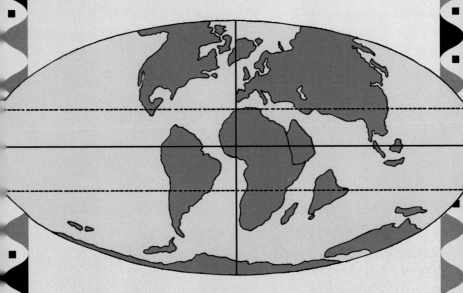

**This map shows the arrangement of the
continents during the time of Gallimimus.**

A nest of dinosaur eggs in the park is supposed to be impossible! Dr. Wu, the genetic engineer at Jurassic Park, said all the dinosaurs created for the Park are female. So how could this happen? Dr. Grant examines the eggshells carefully.

Gallimimus and its close cousin Struthiomimus belong to a group of dinosaurs known as Ornithomimids. Scientists often compare them to ostriches. In fact, Struthiomimus means "ostrich-imitator." These dinosaurs resemble the modern flightless bird, although it is very unlikely they are directly related. Ostrich dinosaurs, like ostriches today, could run at high speed.

The size of an adult Gallimimus compared to a six-foot (1.85 m) human.

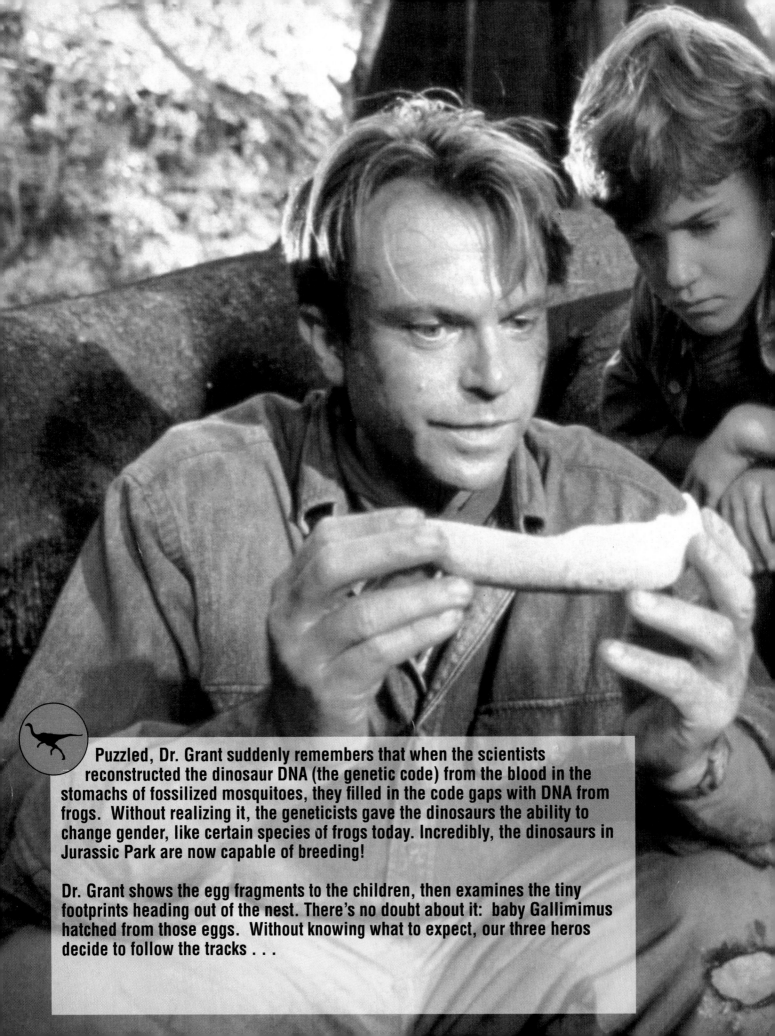

Puzzled, Dr. Grant suddenly remembers that when the scientists reconstructed the dinosaur DNA (the genetic code) from the blood in the stomachs of fossilized mosquitoes, they filled in the code gaps with DNA from frogs. Without realizing it, the geneticists gave the dinosaurs the ability to change gender, like certain species of frogs today. Incredibly, the dinosaurs in Jurassic Park are now capable of breeding!

Dr. Grant shows the egg fragments to the children, then examines the tiny footprints heading out of the nest. There's no doubt about it: baby Gallimimus hatched from those eggs. Without knowing what to expect, our three heros decide to follow the tracks . . .

Gallimimus fossils are found in rock deposits throughout central Asia. Its North American cousin, Struthiomimus, lived about the same time in the western interior of Canada, the United States and Mexico. Like many dinosaurs during the last part of the dinosaur age, ostrich dinosaurs are believed to have migrated from Asia into North America across a land bridge that linked the two continents during this time.

This map shows where the bones of Gallimimus and its North American cousin Struthiomimus have been found.

Gallimimus lived in semi-arid forest and sandy desert. Struthiomimus lived in many different North American environments, but most specimens have been found in the river delta deposits of western Canada.

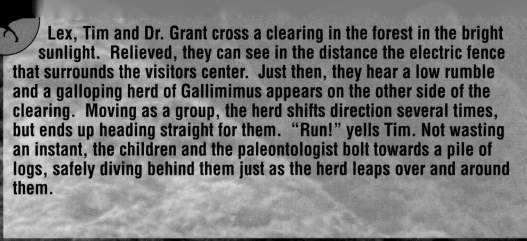

Lex, Tim and Dr. Grant cross a clearing in the forest in the bright sunlight. Relieved, they can see in the distance the electric fence that surrounds the visitors center. Just then, they hear a low rumble and a galloping herd of Gallimimus appears on the other side of the clearing. Moving as a group, the herd shifts direction several times, but ends up heading straight for them. "Run!" yells Tim. Not wasting an instant, the children and the paleontologist bolt towards a pile of logs, safely diving behind them just as the herd leaps over and around them.

This illustration compares the foot of a Gallimimus (left) and one of an ostrich (right).

Notice how similar they are. Both are made to absorb impact with the ground while the animal is running at high speed. The ostrich has only two toes, while the Gallimimus has three. Ostriches lost the third toe during their evolution. When scientists examined fossil footprints made by North American ostrich dinosaurs, they discovered the inside toe barely touched the ground when the dinosaur ran.

Some scientists have suggested that ostrich dinosaurs used their long and slender fingers to dig for insects and pick fruit. Others think they were active hunters that used their long fingers to skewer small mammals and other animals. No one knows which theory is correct. Indeed, they may have been used for something else. In paleontology, there are still many mysteries.

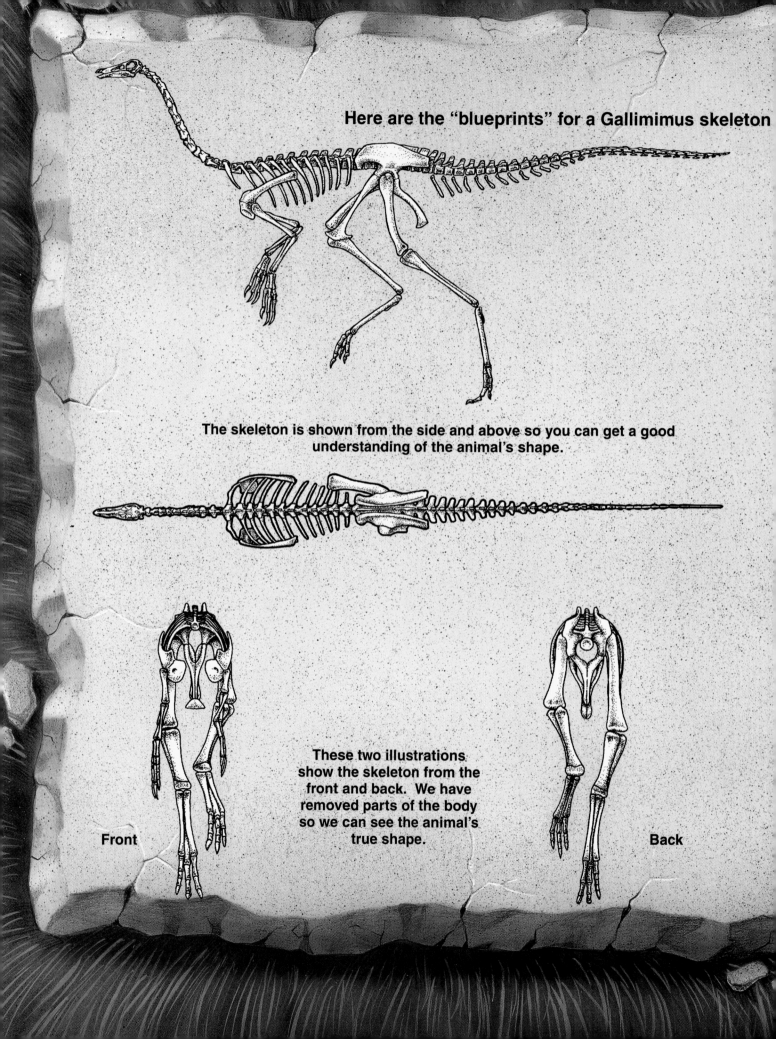

Here are the "blueprints" for a Gallimimus skeleton

The skeleton is shown from the side and above so you can get a good understanding of the animal's shape.

These two illustrations show the skeleton from the front and back. We have removed parts of the body so we can see the animal's true shape.

Front

Back

and the muscles that cover its bones.

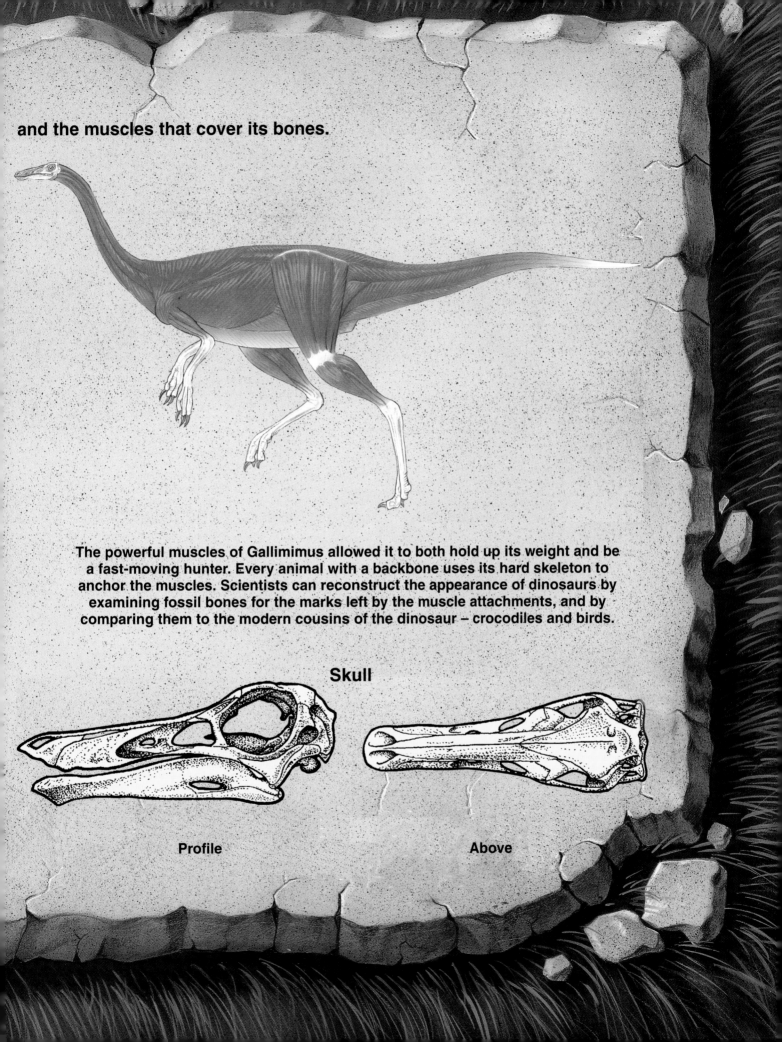

The powerful muscles of Gallimimus allowed it to both hold up its weight and be a fast-moving hunter. Every animal with a backbone uses its hard skeleton to anchor the muscles. Scientists can reconstruct the appearance of dinosaurs by examining fossil bones for the marks left by the muscle attachments, and by comparing them to the modern cousins of the dinosaur – crocodiles and birds.

Skull

Profile

Above

Our heros breathe a sigh of relief. Suddenly, the escaped Tyrannosaurus thunders out of the forest and grabs a Gallimimus in its powerful jaws. The Gallimimus herd runs away "squawking" in panic. This clearing is definitely dangerous, and Dr. Grant and the kids quietly slip away, hopefully out of sight of the fearsome T. rex.

This illustration shows the skeleton of Struthiomimus, a cousin of Gallimimus, as it was found in Alberta, Canada.

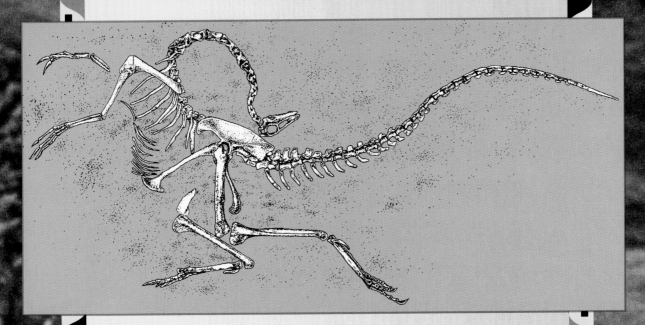

Here is the skeleton of a Struthiomimus as it was found in the badlands of Dinosaur Provincial Park in southern Alberta, Canada. Notice that the skeleton is in a rather uncomfortable position. The head and neck are pulled back and its legs appear frozen in mid-stride. Scientists have often found ostrich dinosaurs in this position. It is believed to have been caused by the tightening and shortening of the animal's powerful tendons soon after death. The tendons pulled the legs up and the neck back, a process frequently observed in dead bodies of many types of long-necked animals today.

The senses of Gallimimus were very sharp. Its huge eyes were used to survey its territory and a large part of its brain was devoted to coordinating signals from the eyes. Due to the size of its eyes, some researchers have suggested that Gallimimus was nocturnal. As Gallimimus was closely related to Tyrannosaurus, it probably shared its excellent hunting abilities.

Gallimimus had no teeth. Indeed, its sharp bird-like beak appears to have been almost as efficient as a set of teeth. We don't often remember that hawks, eagles and owls use only their beaks to pull apart and eat their prey.

DANGER
10,000 VOLTS

At last, they are nearing the electric fence enclosing the visitors compound. Dr. Grant is relieved to see the power warning lights are off, which means the fence is still shut down and they can climb over it without risking a 10,000 volt zap. Hearing the roar of the Tyrannosaurus in the distance, they quickly start climbing.

They don't know that at this very moment Dr. Sattler is trying to get the security system on. Suddenly, lights on the electric fence start flashing and an alarm sounds, warning that the power will soon be back on. There's no time to lose! Lex and Dr. Grant jump down the other side of the fence, but Tim slips and is too terrified to move. Dr. Grant and Lex shout at him to jump and run, but Tim is too scared to let go! What's going to happen to Tim?

Gallimimus probably ate a wide variety of foods.
While the main course was probably small animals,
it may have balanced its diet with fruit and plants.

Mammals

The wide variety of cat-sized
mammals that shared the world
with Gallimimus were all
probably on its menu! With
swift and sharp-clawed hands,
Gallimimus was capable of
capturing all kinds of small
animals.

Invertebrates

This refers to everything in the
"bug-to-slug" category animals
with no backbone. No doubt,
Gallimimus snacked on any
ground or flying insects it could
catch.

Baby Dinosaurs

Some paleontologists feel
the Gallimimus also ate baby
dinosaurs. Their sharp claws
would have let them capture baby
dinosaurs easily, escaping from
the mother dinosaur's fury at high
speed.

PREHISTORIC DESSERT

You need:

1/2 slice of watermelon
3 strawberries
1 raisin
1 banana
1 round slice of orange
2 kiwis

Place the watermelon slice on a plate. Cut strawberries in half and place along
the rind of the watermelon to make the dinosaur's spines. Cut the orange slice in half.
Use one half to make the dinosaur's head, placing a raisin for the eye.
Cut a piece off the other half to make the tail (eat what's left over).

To make the legs, peel the banana, cut in half and in half again, lengthwise.
Place the banana legs below the watermelon. Slice the kiwis and overlap on the plate as
vegetation. Once your prehistoric dessert is finished you can eat it!

Bipedal	An animal that walks on its two back legs.
Carnivore	Any animal that derives most of its food from animal flesh.
DNA	The short name for the genetic blueprints that determine the structure of a living organism.
Dinosaur	An extinct group of land-dwelling animals closely related to birds and reptiles.
Embryo	A fertilized animal egg.
Fossil	Any preserved evidence of ancient life.
Nocturnal	An animal that spends most of its time active at night.
Paleontologist	A scientist who studies the evidence of ancient life.
Paleobotanist	A scientist who specifically studies fossil plants.
Predator	Any organism that pursues or hunts animals for food.
Saurischian	One of the two main groups of dinosaurs, defined by the position of the bones in their hips. The bone positions resemble those of modern lizards, therefore they are called "lizard-hipped" or Saurischian.
Tendon	The soft tissue structure used to attach muscles to bones.

Text
Lucie Duchesne and Andrew Leitch

Research
Andrew Leitch

Cover Illustration
Michel-Thomas Poulin

Illustrations
PaleoImage Ltd.

Art Direction
Studio de la Montagne
Louis C. Hébert

Desktop Publishing
Benoît Lafond and Line Godbout

Produced by
Group Potential Inc.

With photos from the movie
Jurassic Park

From a screenplay by
Michael Crichton et David Koepp

Based on a novel by
Michael Crichton

© Les Éditions Nublar Enr. All rights reserved. Printed in Canada.
TM & © 1993 Universal Studios, Inc. & Amblin Entertainment, Inc. All rights reserved.
JURASSIC PARK and JURASSIC PARK logo are registered trademarks of Universal City
Studios, Inc. & Amblin Entertainment, Inc.
Legal deposit Bibliothèque nationale du Québec, 1993.
Legal deposit Nationale Library of Canada,1993. ISBN 2-921602-11-3

IN THIS COLLECTION